SCHOLASTIC

READ & RESPOND

Bringing the best books to life in the classroom

Activities based on
The Secret Garden
By Frances Hodgson Burnett

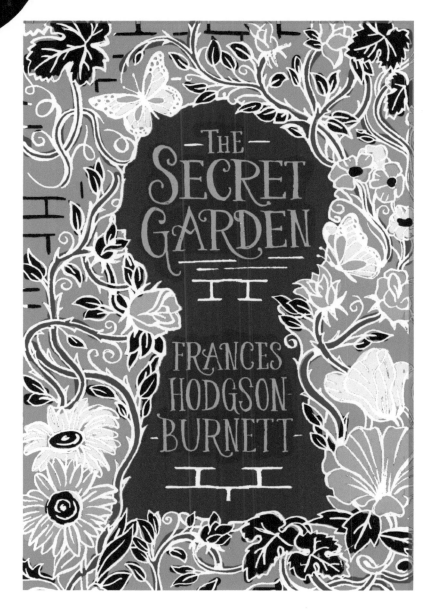

FOR AGES 7–11

Published in the UK by Scholastic Education, 2020
Book End, Range Road, Witney, Oxfordshire, OX29 0YD
A division of Scholastic Limited
London – New York – Toronto – Sydney - Auckland
Mexico City – New Delhi – Hong Kong

Printed and bound by Ashford Colour Press
© 2020 Scholastic Ltd
1 2 3 4 5 6 7 8 9   0 1 2 3 4 5 6 7 8 9

British Library Cataloguing-in-Publication Data
A catalogue record for this book is available from the British Library.
ISBN 978-1407-18324-4

Extracts from *The National Curriculum in England, English Programme of Study* © Crown Copyright. Reproduced under the terms of the Open Government Licence (OGL). http://www.nationalarchives.gov.uk/doc/open-government-licence/version/3

Authors Jillian Powell
Editorial team Rachel Morgan, Vicki Yates, Suzanne Adams, Julia Roberts
Series designer Dipa Mistry
Typesetter QBS Learning
Illustrator Alessandra Santelli

Acknowledgements
The publishers gratefully acknowledge permission to reproduce the following copyright material: Scholastic Children's Books for permission to use the cover from *The Secret Garden* written by Frances Hodgson Burnett (Scholastic Children's Books, 2019). Reproduced with permission of Scholastic Children's Books. All rights reserved.

Photograph Page 18: The Yorkshire Moors, Alamy

Every effort has been made to trace copyright holders for the works reproduced in this book, and the publishers apologise for any inadvertent omissions.

How to use Read & Respond in your classroom...

Read & Respond provides teaching ideas related to a specific well-loved children's book. Each Read & Respond book is divided into the following sections:

ABOUT THE BOOK AND AUTHOR

Gives you some background information about the book and the author.

GUIDED READING

Breaks the book down into sections and gives notes for using it with guided reading groups. A bookmark has been provided on page 12 containing comprehension questions. The children can be directed to refer to these as they read.

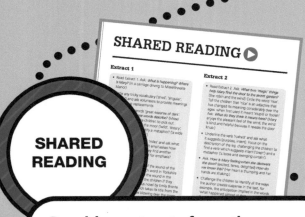

SHARED READING

Provides extracts from the children's book with associated notes for focused work. There is also one non-fiction extract that relates to the children's book.

GRAMMAR, PUNCTUATION & SPELLING

Provides word-level work related to the children's book so you can teach grammar, punctuation and spelling in context.

PLOT, CHARACTER & SETTING

Contains activity ideas focused on the plot, characters and the setting of the story.

GET WRITING

Provides writing activities related to the children's book. These activities may be based directly on the children's book or be broadly based on the themes and concepts of the story.

Has speaking and listening activities related to the children's book. These activities may be based directly on the children's book or be broadly based on the themes and concepts of the story.

TALK ABOUT IT

ASSESSMENT

Contains short activities that will help you assess whether the children have understood concepts and curriculum objectives. They are designed to be informal activities to feed into your planning.

II The titles are great fun to use and cover exactly the range of books that children most want to read. It makes it easy to explore texts fully and ensure the children want to keep on reading more. *II*

Chris Flanagan, Year 5 Teacher, St Thomas of Canterbury Primary School

Activities

The activities follow the same format:

- **Objective:** the objective for the lesson. It will be based upon a curriculum objective, but will often be more specific to the focus being covered.

- **What you need:** a list of resources you need to teach the lesson, including photocopiable pages.

- **What to do:** the activity notes.

- **Differentiation:** this is provided where specific and useful differentiation advice can be given to support and/or extend the learning in the activity. Differentiation by providing additional adult support has not been included as this will be at a teacher's discretion based upon specific children's needs and ability, as well as the availability of support.

The activities are numbered for reference within each section and should move through the text sequentially – so you can use the lesson while you are reading the book. Once you have read the book, most of the activities can be used in any order you wish.

▼ CURRICULUM LINKS

Section	Activity	Curriculum objectives
Guided reading		Comprehension: To ask questions to improve their understanding.
Shared reading	1	Comprehension: To discuss and evaluate how authors use language, including figurative language, considering the impact on the reader.
	2	Comprehension: To identify how language, structure and presentation contribute to meaning.
	3	Comprehension: To check that the book makes sense to them, discussing their understanding and exploring the meaning of words in context; to provide reasoned justifications for their views.
	4	Comprehension: To discuss and evaluate how authors use language, including figurative language, considering the impact on the reader.
Grammar, punctuation & spelling	1	Vocabulary, grammar and punctuation: To use relative clauses beginning with who, which, where, when, whose, that or with an implied (i.e. omitted) relative pronoun.
	2	Vocabulary, grammar and punctuation: To use expanded noun phrases to convey complicated information concisely.
	3	Vocabulary, grammar and punctuation: To use passive verbs to affect the presentation of information in a sentence.
	4	Vocabulary, grammar and punctuation: To use the perfect form of verbs to mark relationships of time.
	5	Vocabulary, grammar and punctuation: To use modal verbs or adverbs to indicate degrees of possibility.
	6	Vocabulary, grammar and punctuation: To use brackets, dashes or commas to indicate parenthesis.
Plot, character & setting	1	Comprehension: To summarise the main ideas drawn from more than one paragraph, identifying key details that support the main ideas.
	2	Comprehension: To draw inferences such as inferring characters' feelings, thoughts and motives from their actions, and justifying inferences with evidence.
	3	Comprehension: To make comparisons within and across books.
	4	Composition: To use further organisational and presentational devices to structure text and to guide the reader (for example, headings, bullet points, underlining).
	5	Comprehension: To make comparisons within books.
	6	Comprehension: To draw inferences such as inferring characters' feelings, thoughts and motives from their actions, and justifying inferences with evidence.
	7	Comprehension: To identify how language, structure and presentation contribute to meaning.
	8	Comprehension: To identify and discuss themes and conventions in and across a wide range of writing.

Section	Activity	Curriculum objectives
Talk about it	1	Spoken language: To speak audibly and fluently with an increasing command of Standard English.
	2	Spoken language: To maintain attention and participate actively in collaborative conversations, staying on topic and initiating and responding to comments.
	3	Spoken language: To use spoken language to develop understanding through speculating, hypothesising, imagining and exploring ideas.
	4	Spoken language: To give well-structured descriptions, explanations and narratives for different purposes, including for expressing feelings.
	5	Spoken language: To participate in discussions and debates.
	6	Spoken language: To select and use appropriate registers for effective communication.
Get writing	1	Comprehension: To summarise the main ideas drawn from more than one paragraph.
	2	Composition: To plan their writing by identifying the audience for and purpose of the writing, selecting the appropriate form and using other similar writing as models for their own.
	3	Composition: To identify the audience for and purpose of the writing, selecting the appropriate form and using other similar writing as models for their own.
	4	Composition: To use organisational and presentational devices to structure text and guide the reader (headings, bullet points, underlining).
	5	Comprehension: To discuss and evaluate how authors use language, including figurative language, considering the impact on the reader.
	6	Composition: To note and develop initial ideas, drawing on reading and research where necessary.
Assessment	1	Comprehension: To ask questions to improve their understanding.
	2	Comprehension: To provide reasoned justifications for their views.
	3	Comprehension: To check that the book makes sense to them, discussing their understanding and exploring the meaning of words in context. Vocabulary, grammar and punctuation: To use brackets, dashes or commas to indicate parenthesis.
	4	Comprehension: To identify and discuss themes and conventions in and across a wide range of writing.
	5	Spoken language: To give well-structured descriptions, explanations and narratives for different purposes, including for expressing feelings.
	6	Comprehension: To summarise the main ideas drawn from more than one paragraph.

THE SECRET GARDEN

Key facts
The Secret Garden

◉ **Author:**
Frances Hodgson Burnett

◉ **First published:**
1911 by Grosset &
Dunlap, U.S.

◉ **Adaptations:**
First filmed as a silent movie
in 1919, the novel has been
adapted into films, stage
plays, musicals and opera.
The 1949 film version was
filmed in black and white,
with the garden sequences
in colour. A new film based
on the novel, but set in 1947,
will be released in 2020.

◉ **Did you know?**
The garden in the novel was
inspired by a real garden
which the author discovered
in the grounds of an old
manor house in Kent where
she lived for ten years.

About the book

The Secret Garden is a familiar and much-loved children's novel.
First published in serial form in 1910, and as a novel the following
year, it quickly became a best seller. It has since become a children's
classic, translated into many languages and adapted for numerous
television, film and musical versions. The central character, Mary
Lennox, is an orphan who is sent home from India to England after
both her parents die during a cholera epidemic. Uprooted from
everything she is accustomed to, she finds herself living an isolated
and unhappy existence in her uncle's gloomy mansion surrounded
by the wild Yorkshire moors. Mary is a product of her spoiled yet
neglected upbringing: arrogant, selfish and stubborn. Her salvation
comes through her discovery of a secret garden, hidden behind a
locked door in an ivy-clad wall in the mansion grounds. The garden
becomes Mary's escape into a secret world that is both transformative
and healing. Slowly, as the garden unfolds its secrets, Mary begins
to open her heart to emotions and friendships. When she discovers
a sickly boy lying bed-ridden in the mansion and finds out he is her
cousin, she resolves to share the restorative powers of the garden and
nature with him. The novel is redolent of the author's own love of
gardening and nature, as well as her beliefs in the Christian Science,
Spiritualist and New Thought movements. It is a tale of redemption for
the children through the healing power of nature and the outdoors,
making it a relevant and engaging story today, more than a century
after it was written.

About the author

Frances Hodgson Burnett was born in Victorian England, in
Manchester, in 1849. After her father died when she was only
three years old, his hardware business collapsed and his widow and
five children fell on hard times. Frances's only education was at an
elementary dame school but she read and wrote avidly, scribbling
stories on any scrap of paper she could find. In 1865, the family
emigrated to Tennessee in the United States of America to live in a
log cabin with Frances's uncle. Frances, still in her teens, tried to earn
money by setting up a small school, but then found her talent lay
in writing stories for women's magazines. In 1873, she married and
went on to have two sons. The youngest, Vivian, was the inspiration
for her novel *Little Lord Fauntleroy* which was published in 1886. It
quickly became a best-seller, inspiring plays, films and merchandise
from playing cards to toys and clothes. Its success brought a rich and
comfortable lifestyle, however Frances's life was marred by the death
of her eldest son from influenza and the subsequent breakdown of
her marriage. She turned increasingly to Spiritualism, Christian Science
and the New Thought movement which began to provide ideas and
themes for her writing. After her second marriage, she moved to
New York, writing more than 50 novels as well as stories and stage
plays before her death in 1924. Her last public appearance was at the
opening of the film of *Little Lord Fauntleroy*. She once said to her son
Vivian, 'I have tried to write more happiness into the world.'

GUIDED READING ▶

An orphan called Mary

Introduce the book by reading the title and looking for clues to the content and setting (an orphan called Mary, an old mansion, a secret garden). Some children may be familiar with the story from film or television adaptations. Invite the children to offer subjective opinions on why the title sounds engaging or intriguing, without giving away the storyline (the idea of discovering a secret and private place which you can make your own). Read the first chapter together then ask a volunteer to summarise where Mary has been living and what has happened. (She has been living in India, where a cholera outbreak has killed most of the household including both her parents.) Ask the children to suggest words to describe Mary, encouraging them to consider her character as well as her appearance: sickly, selfish, spoiled. Ask: *What do we learn from the first sentence of the novel?* Mary has now left India and has gone to live with her uncle at his manor house. Refer to question 6 on the bookmark. Continue reading through the second chapter. Pause at the verse that Basil sings and explain it comes from an old English nursery rhyme. Ask: *What do you think 'contrary' means?* (difficult, headstrong, wilful) Tell the children that the author's original idea for a title for the novel was *Mistress Mary*. Encourage them to consider question 1 on the bookmark as they read the story.

A new life

Ask the children what else we have learned about Mary's upbringing and relationship with her parents. Can they explain why she is 'contrary' and disagreeable? (Her parents showed no interest and paid no attention to her.) Highlight the fact that Mary is creating a garden as she did earlier in India, noting a key theme suggested by the novel's title.

Review questions 3 and 4 on the bookmark. Invite the children's responses to the prospect of living at Misselthwaite Manor. Continue reading Chapter 3. Pause to note the Yorkshire dialect and words such as 'brougham' (meaning a light, horse-drawn carriage) and remind the children that the novel is set in the early 1900s. Raise questions 8 and 9 on the bookmark. Read as far as '"He doesn't want to see her."' Ask a volunteer to explain who 'he' is and what this suggests. (her uncle, Sir Archibald Craven; he doesn't sound very kind or welcoming)

Changes

Read to the end of Chapter 4. Pause to consider the dialogue between Martha and Mary. Remind the children that the novel was published over a century ago and that it reflects ideas and values of its time – in particular, attitudes among European peoples living in countries like India which were then colonies under the rule of the British Empire. Refer to question 11 on the bookmark. Establish that we may find some views shocking or offensive today because we no longer accept those ideas, attitudes and values. Highlight how Martha is challenging some of the ideas and customs that Mary has grown up believing. Pause at the sentence '"…and as she had never before been interested in anyone but herself, it was the dawning of a healthy sentiment."' Encourage the children to listen out for further signs that Mary will change, and what it is that changes her. Suggest that the robin triggers change in Mary. Ask: *Can you suggest how?* (Mary is curious and interested in him and makes a connection with him; he makes her acknowledge her own loneliness and how it is that which makes her disagreeable or contrary.)

GUIDED READING

A secret kingdom

Highlight the first mention of the secret garden. Ask: *What do we learn about it?* (that it has been locked up for ten years, since the death of Mr Craven's wife) Discuss how Mary is changing – and what changes her – as you read Chapter 5. Ask: *What is the hook that makes us want to read on at the end of the chapter?* (to find out who is crying) Raise question 5 on the bookmark. Read the next chapter at pace, noting how the author builds suspense and mystery. Continue reading to the end of Chapter 8. Pause to note the impact of the final sentence. Read on through the next chapter. Ask: *What does Mary love about the garden?* (It is her own secret kingdom; she finds purpose in helping the plants grow.) Again, consider the ending to the chapter, revisiting question 5 on the bookmark. Read Chapter 9, pausing to ask who is the young lady that Ben Weatherstaff talks about (Mr Craven's late wife). Continue reading to the end of Chapter 12. Ask: *Who might have done some pruning in the garden before Dickon and Mary begin to awaken it?* (Ben Weatherstaff) As you read Chapter 13, note the shift in mood when Mary is summoned to meet Mr Craven. Ask: *Whom do you think Mary reminds him of and why?* (his wife, who also loved gardening)

Colin Craven

Continue reading Chapter 13, pausing at the beginning to note the shift back indoors and to the mysterious crying sound. At the end of the chapter, discuss how Colin is in some ways similar to how Mary was (sickly, spoiled) but how she has changed since discovering the garden. Explore this idea further as you read through the next few chapters. Suggest Colin may have met his match in Mary and challenge the children to explain how. (She is equally stubborn and wilful.) Highlight the way Dickon has opened Mary's eyes to the healing power of nature and now she is doing the same for Colin. Raise question 12 on the bookmark. Pause at the end of Chapter 16 to ask what has altered Mary's mood and why she has changed her mind about seeing Colin. (Mr Craven's gifts have cheered her up and she begins to understand the reason for Colin's behaviour.)

Ask: *Why do you think that standing up to Colin, as Mary does, is just what he needs? Is the illness in his mind or his body?* Encourage the children to give reasons. Continue reading Chapter 19, pausing to ask what the cook means when she says Colin has '"found his master"'. (Mary is the only one able to command him.)

A kind of magic

Read on through the next few chapters, pausing in Chapter 21 to question the significance of the dead tree in the garden with the broken branch. (Colin's mother died after she fell from the tree.) Ask: *How does the robin perform Magic?* (He helpfully provides distraction when Colin asks about the tree.) *Can you recall an earlier time when the robin performed Magic?* (When he showed Mary the key to the garden door.) *What other kind of Magic happens at the end of the chapter?* (Colin is able to stand unaided for the first time.) Can they explain how this happens? (Ben Weatherstaff provokes him, making him determined to prove he is not a cripple.) Again, point out how his thoughts and feelings affect his body. Link to question 2 on the bookmark. Read to the end of Chapter 22, pausing to ask why Ben Weatherstaff may have chosen a rose for Colin to plant. (His mother especially loved roses.) Begin reading Chapter 23. Suggest that the meaning of the word 'queer' is similar to 'contrary' in this context. Point out that the meaning of words can change over time, reminding them that the story was written in the early 1900s. Raise question 10 on the bookmark. At the end of the chapter, discuss the idea behind the concept of Magic that Colin is proposing to study: that *willing* something to happen can make it happen. Note the way the author links this concept to the practice of *fakirs* (holy men) in India. Re-visit questions 2 and 4 on the bookmark. Suggest that these ideas are very resonant today in many faiths and belief systems. Read the next chapter, pausing to ask the children to summarise what is making Colin better physically (walking, exercises) and mentally (the Magic, laughter). Link to question 15 on the bookmark. As you begin reading Chapter 25, ask question 13 on the bookmark.

Restoration and renewal

Read on as far as the beginning of Chapter 27. As you read, extract key themes: the power of thoughts over physical health and the introduction of more explicitly Christian/religious ideas: the idea of a 'joy maker' (God) and the Magic of his creation. Consider question 14 on the bookmark. As you read the last chapter, note the shift in location and the focus of the narrative to Mr Craven on his travels in Europe. Return to question 6 on the bookmark. Ask: *How does the Magic now affect Mr Craven?* (He suddenly feels renewed, at the very moment Colin is realising he is well at last.) Ask a volunteer to explain the significance of the words 'In the garden', when Mrs Medlock tells Mr Craven where he will find his son. (They are the same words his wife said to him in his dream.) Pause, as you read the last paragraphs, to note how the author summarises the plot as Colin explains to his father how he has been restored to health. Highlight the theme of healing, noting that it is not just Colin but also Mary, Mr Craven and the garden that have been restored and renewed. Discuss question 7 on the bookmark. Encourage subjective responses to the story ending.

The Secret Garden
by Frances Hodgson Burnett

Focus on...
Meaning

1. What does the nursery rhyme tell us about Mary and how others see her?

2. What role does 'Magic' play in the story?

3. How are gardens and gardening important to Mary?

Focus on...
Organisation

4. How does the author create links between India and Yorkshire in England?

5. How does the author use hooks at chapter ends to make us want to read on?

6. When does the location shift to drive the plot forwards?

7. How do the seasons help shape the plot of the story?

The Secret Garden
by Frances Hodgson Burnett

Focus on...
Language and features

8. What does the use of Yorkshire dialect contribute to the story?

9. Which words in the story tell us that it is set in the past?

10. Which words used in the story have a different meaning today?

Focus on...
Purpose, viewpoints and effects

11. Which views or attitudes expressed in the story are very different from today's?

12. What is the author's message about gardens and the natural world?

13. How does the viewpoint change in Chapter 25?

14. How does religion feature in the story?

15. Who or what provides humour in the story?

SHARED READING ▶

Extract 1

- Read Extract 1. Ask: *What is happening? Where is Mary?* (in a carriage driving to Misselthwaite Manor)

- Circle any tricky vocabulary ('shed', 'singular', 'dreary') and ask volunteers to provide meanings and suggest replacements.

- Underline the words 'great expanse of dark'. Ask: *What do these words describe?* (Missel Moor) Challenge the children to pick out adjectives describing the moor ('wild', 'dreary', 'bleak'). Can they identify a metaphor? ('a wide expanse of black ocean')

- Circle the repeated word 'miles' and ask what effect the repetition has (It emphasises how huge the moor is.) Can they find another example of repetition used for emphasis? ('On and on…')

- Focus on the description of the sound of the wind. Can they recall which word in Yorkshire dialect is used to describe the sound in the novel? ('wuthering') Ask the children if they have heard of the famous novel by Emily Bronte *Wuthering Heights* which takes its title from the sound the wind makes blowing over the moor.

- Ask: *What is Mrs Medlock's opinion of the moor?* (She thinks it is a dreary, wild place.) She says there are 'plenty who like it'. Can they name someone in the novel who likes the moor? (Dickon)

- Underline Mrs Medlock's description '"…and nothing lives on but wild ponies and sheep"'. Ask: *Do you think this is correct?* Encourage the children to give reasons. *How does Dickon view the moor?* (as a wild and exciting place, bursting with life)

Extract 2

- Read Extract 2. Ask: *What two 'magic' things help Mary find the door to the secret garden?* (the robin and the wind) Circle the word 'nice'. Tell the children that 'nice' is an adjective that has changed its meaning considerably over the ages: when first used it meant 'stupid or foolish'. Ask: *What do they think it means here?* (Mary enjoys the pleasant feel of the wind; the wind is kind and helpful because it reveals the door knob.)

- Underline the verb 'rushed' and ask what it suggests (purpose, intent). Focus on the description of the ivy, challenging the children to find a verb which suggests intent ('crept') and a metaphor ('a loose and swinging curtain').

- Ask: *How is Mary feeling when she discovers the door?* (excited, tense, delighted) *How do we know this?* (Her heart is thumping and her hands are shaking.)

- Challenge the children to identify all the ways the author creates suspense in the text, for example, the anticipation implied in the words 'what happened almost at that moment…' and the use of a question 'What was this under her hands…?'

- Encourage the children to examine the word order in two of the sentences: 'This she did…'; 'Thick as the ivy hung…'. Ask: *What effect does the author create?* Establish that the word order helps us to experience the suspense and excitement at the same time as Mary.

- Ask: *Why does Mary takes a long breath?* (to steady her nerves, because she is afraid of being discovered before she can see inside the garden)

SHARED READING

Extract 3

- Read Extract 3. Ask a volunteer to summarise the belief or theory that the author presents in the text: that our mind and its thoughts affect the health of our physical body. Underline the words 'the last century'. Ask: *Which century is the author referring to?* (the 19th century, because her novel was written in 1910)

- Circle tricky words ('wretched', 'detestation', 'hysterical', 'hypochondriac'). Challenge the children to explain meanings or suggest replacements.

- Focus on the adjectives used to describe Mary and Colin and their thoughts before they change ('disagreeable', 'sickly', 'bored', 'wretched', 'hysterical', 'hideous'). Discuss which words suggest how they are seen by others, and which words suggest how they feel themselves. Can they suggest why Mary might appear yellow? (An unhealthy liver can make the skin look yellow.)

- Challenge the children to pick out examples of alliteration ('hysterical, half-crazy little hypochondriac') and a simile ('like a flood').

- Explore implied meaning in the text. Ask: *How did circumstances push Mary about?* (Her parents died so she moved to England to live at the manor.) Invite volunteers to explain each reference to characters or places in the story: 'moorland cottages' (Susan Sowerby's cottage), 'crabbed old gardeners' (Ben Weatherstaff), 'common little Yorkshire housemaids' (Martha), 'the moor boy' (Dickon), 'and his "creatures"' (all the animals that he talks to and tames).

- Encourage the children to offer subjective opinions on the author's argument. Ask: *Do you think our thoughts can affect our body's health?* Introduce the phrase 'holistic health' and explain that many experts today believe that the health of the mind and the body are connected.

Extract 4

- Read Extract 4.

- Circle tricky words or phrases ('shrouded', 'vibrant', 'dense', 'majestic', 'prey', 'venomous', 'forged', 'bio-diverse habitat') and ask volunteers to suggest meaning and/or replacements. Encourage the children to use their knowledge of word roots to help them. They may know what a shroud or a forge is and be able to guess the meaning of the verb from the noun, or they may know the noun 'majesty' and so guess the meaning of the adjective.

- Challenge them to identify figurative language, including metaphors, which describe the heather as a work of art ('vibrant tapestry', 'patchwork').

- Ask the children to cite all the new facts they learn about moorland from the text, listing them on the board. Repeat the exercise, extracting ideas about moorland found in the novel. Compare and contrast the two lists, identifying which facts about moorland appear in the novel (the variety of wildlife, the blooming of the heather in summer and so on).

- Challenge the children to suggest a descriptive phrase about the moor which reflects how Mrs Medlock sees it (wild and windswept). Explore which ideas contained in the text reflect Dickon's view of the moor. (the fact that it is alive with plants and wildlife) Focus on the phrase 'bio-diverse habitat'. Encourage the children to explain how the plant and animal species that live on the moor depend on each other (the plants provide cover and food for animals; the animals pollinate the plants and provide food for other species). How do the children think the novel reflects this idea?

Extract 1

The carriage lamps shed a yellow light on a rough-looking road which seemed to be cut through bushes and low-growing things which ended in the great expanse of dark apparently spread out before and around them. A wind was rising and making a singular, wild, low, rushing sound.

"It's – it's not the sea, is it?" said Mary, looking round at her companion.

"No, not it," answered Mrs Medlock. "Nor it isn't fields nor mountains, it's just miles and miles and miles of wild land that nothing grows on but heather and gorse and broom, and nothing lives on but wild ponies and sheep."

"I feel as if it might be the sea, if there were water on it," said Mary. "It sounds like the sea just now."

"That's the wind blowing through the bushes," Mrs Medlock said. "It's a wild, dreary enough place to my mind, though there's plenty that likes it – particularly when the heather's in bloom."

On and on they drove through the darkness, and though the rain stopped, the wind rushed by and whistled and made strange sounds. The road went up and down, and several times the carriage passed over a little bridge beneath which water rushed very fast with a great deal of noise. Mary felt as if the drive would never come to an end and that the wide, bleak moor was a wide expanse of black ocean through which she was passing on a strip of dry land.

"I don't like it," she said to herself. "I don't like it," and she pinched her thin lips more tightly together.

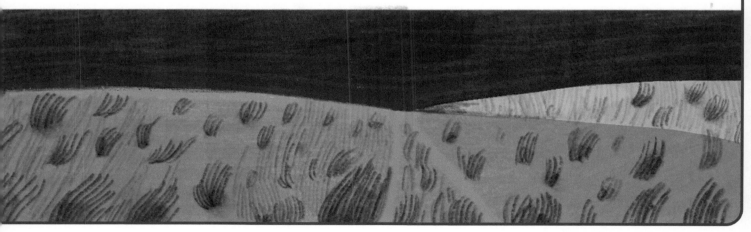

Extract 2

Mary Lennox had heard a great deal about Magic in her Ayah's stories, and she always said that what happened almost at that moment was Magic.

One of the nice little gusts of wind rushed down the walk, and it was a stronger one than the rest. It was strong enough to wave the branches of the trees, and it was more than strong enough to sway the trailing sprays of untrimmed ivy hanging from the wall. Mary had stepped close to the robin, and suddenly the gust of wind swung aside some loose ivy trails, and more suddenly still she jumped towards it and caught it in her hand. This she did because she had seen something under it – a round knob which had been covered by the leaves hanging over it. It was the knob of a door.

She put her hands under the leaves and began to pull and push them aside. Thick as the ivy hung, it nearly all was a loose and swinging curtain, though some had crept over wood and iron. Mary's heart began to thump and her hands to shake a little in her delight and excitement. The robin kept singing and twittering away and tilting his head on one side, as if he were as excited as she was. What was this under her hands which was square and made of iron and which her fingers found a hole in?

It was the lock of the door which had been closed ten years and she put her hand in her pocket, drew out the key and found it fitted the keyhole. She put the key in and turned it. It took two hands to do it, but it did turn.

And then she took a long breath and looked behind her up the Long Walk to see if anyone was coming.

Extract 3

One of the new things people began to find out in the last century was that thoughts – just mere thoughts – are as powerful as electric batteries – as good for one as sunlight is, or as bad for one as poison. To let a sad thought or a bad one get into your mind is as dangerous as letting a scarlet fever germ get into your body. If you let it stay there after it has got in, you may never get over it as long as you live.

So long as Mistress Mary's mind was full of disagreeable thoughts about her dislikes and sour opinions of people and her determination not to be pleased by or interested in anything, she was a yellow-faced, sickly, bored and wretched child. Circumstances, however, were very kind to her, though she was not at all aware of it. They began to push her about for her own good. When her mind gradually filled itself with robins, and moorland cottages crowded with children, with queer crabbed old gardeners and common little Yorkshire housemaids, with springtime and with secret gardens coming alive day by day, and also with a moor boy and his "creatures", there was no room left for the disagreeable thoughts which affected her liver and her digestion and made her yellow and tired.

So long as Colin shut himself up in his room and thought only of his fears and weakness and his detestation of people who looked at him and reflected hourly on humps and early death, he was a hysterical, half-crazy little hypochondriac who knew nothing of the sunshine and the spring and also did not know that he could get well and could stand upon his feet if he tried to do it. When new beautiful thoughts began to push out the old hideous ones, life began to come back to him, his blood ran healthily through his veins, and strength poured into him like a flood.

Extract 4

By Jillian Powell

[Voice-over to a film about heather moorland]

Windswept and wild in winter, when they are often shrouded in mist or cloud or dusted with snow, the moors come alive in summer. From July onwards, the local heather or 'ling' flushes pink and purple, cloaking the land in a vibrant tapestry that stretches as far as the eye can see. An evergreen shrub with twiggy stems and tiny bell-like flowers, heather has a dense, low-growing habit and narrow, needle-like leaves to protect it and retain moisture when strong winds sweep across the moors. Traditionally used to make besom brooms for sweeping floors and paths, heather has also been used for tanning leather and dyeing wool. Its nectar provides food for insects, moths and butterflies and is the source of the highly-prized heather honey. Local beekeepers often bring their hives onto the moors in late summer when the heather is in bloom. Sheep and deer graze its growing tips, and red grouse feed on its seeds in winter.

Heather moorland is a patchwork of vegetation: wet heath, dry heath and blanket bog. Many bird species nest, breed and feed on the moors, including the skylark, short-eared owl, golden plover and even the majestic hen harrier. Low-growing plants including coconut-scented gorse, heather, bilberry and crowberry provide dense cover for field mice, voles, lizards and other small mammals which, in turn, provide prey for the adder, Britain's only venomous snake. Heather moorland is a special place, forged by nature and managed by generations of farmers and landowners. The richly bio-diverse habitat is one of the rarest in the world, but an amazing 75% of it is to be found in the UK.

GRAMMAR, PUNCTUATION & SPELLING ▶

1. Useful relatives

Objective
To use relative clauses to join sentences.

What you need
Copies of *The Secret Garden*, flash cards with names of characters or subjects from the novel (Mary, Colin, Dickon, Martha, the secret garden, Misselthwaite Manor, the robin).

What to do

- Arrange the class into pairs. Hand each pair a flash card with a character or topic from the novel.

- Tell each pair to write down a pair of short sentences about their subject. They can refer to the novel to help them. Model one pair of sentences on the board: 'The robin lives in the garden.' 'The robin shows Mary the key to the door.'

- When they have written their sentences, list on the board the relative pronouns: 'who', 'which', 'where', 'when', 'whose', 'that'. Explain to the children that they are now going to try joining their sentences using a relative pronoun. Demonstrate on the board by writing: 'The robin, which lives in the garden, shows Mary the key to the door.'

- Allow the pairs time to write a sentence using a relative pronoun. Let pairs swap their flash cards then repeat the exercise.

- When they have finished, invite pairs to read aloud their sentences. Are there any pronouns that have not been used? If so, encourage pairs to choose a character or topic and compose a sentence aloud using that pronoun.

Differentiation
Support: As a class, draft pairs of short sentences then ask pairs of children to try joining them.

Extension: Challenge pairs to use all the listed pronouns.

2. Expanding nouns

Objective
To use expanded noun phrases to convey complicated information concisely.

What you need
Copies of *The Secret Garden*, Extract 4, photocopiable page 22 'Expanding nouns'.

What to do

- Display an enlarged copy of Extract 4. Re-read the extract together, then circle the words 'flowers', 'leaves', 'plants'. Ask: *Can you identify which part of speech these words are?* (nouns)

- Examine the phrases which expand the nouns to describe them further: 'tiny, bell-like flowers'; 'narrow, needle-like leaves'; 'low-growing plants'. Tell the children that we call this kind of phrase an expanded noun phrase. It is a neat, concise way of telling us more about the subject (noun).

- Challenge the children to find other expanded noun phrases in the extract, underlining or circling them ('dense, low-growing habit', 'richly bio-diverse habitat' and so on).

- Arrange the children into pairs and hand out photocopiable page 22 'Expanding nouns'. Allow them time to fill it in then bring the class back together to review their work. Discuss their process of working, noting that although some phrases may work with more than one noun, (for example, 'The most disagreeable-looking' works with 'face', 'place' and 'child') they might then result in other matches which do not work.

- Ask volunteers to read aloud their sentences, inviting constructive feedback on their noun phrases.

Differentiation
Support: Provide a list of nouns taken from the novel and challenge children to compose noun phrases describing them.

Extension: Challenge children to write more noun phrases describing different nouns they have chosen from the novel.

3. Passive power

Objective
To use passive verbs to affect the presentation of information in a sentence.

What you need
Copies of *The Secret Garden*.

What to do

- Write on the board two sentences: 'Dickon wheeled Colin to the garden.' 'Colin was wheeled to the garden by Dickon.'

- Underline the active and passive verbs. Ask: *What difference does the verb form make to the sense or meaning of the sentence?* (The active puts the emphasis on Dickon who is pushing the chair, the passive puts the emphasis on Colin who is being pushed in the chair.) Reflect that the word 'passive' as an adjective suggests doing nothing or being inactive. Ask: *Which sentence best conveys Colin's lack of activity?* (the passive: the action is being done by someone else) Suggest that in this way, passive verbs can sometimes be a useful way of conveying or reinforcing the meaning.

- Write on the board: 'Martha dressed Mary.' Ask a volunteer to change the verb to passive, writing the new sentence on the board: 'Mary was dressed by Martha.' Again, ask the children which verb form best reflects Mary's helplessness. (the passive)

- Arrange the children into pairs and challenge them to compose more sentences about Mary or Colin using the passive form of the verb to suggest how helpless and spoiled they both are at the beginning of the story.

- Bring the class back together and ask volunteers to read aloud their sentences. Write some of the best suggestions on the board.

Differentiation
Support: Provide a list of sentences with active verbs for children to convert to passive.

Extension: Challenge pairs to write more sentences about other characters (Mr Craven, Ben Weatherstaff) using the passive to help convey meaning.

4. Back in time

Objective
To use the perfect form of verbs to mark relationships of time.

What you need
Copies of *The Secret Garden*.

What to do

- Re-read together the opening paragraph of Chapter 15. Focus on the verb 'had been' in the sentence 'Though there had been no chance…', identifying the past perfect tense (the perfect form *had* plus the past participle *been*). Ask the children what effect this form of the verb has? (It shifts the narrative back in time to things that have happened before the events of the main narrative.) Challenge them to find and read out more past perfect verbs in the paragraph ('had not seemed', 'had spent', 'had looked at', 'had read').

- Discuss the purpose of using the past perfect tense here. (It summarises everything Mary and Colin have been doing during the past week without going into unnecessary or repetitive detail.)

- Arrange the children into pairs. Provide a list of chapters (2, 14, 17, 19, 23) and ask pairs to identify examples of the past perfect tense and discuss their effect and purpose. How does the narrative shift back in time and what action is summarised?

- Challenge each pair to draft up to six sentences about action in the novel using past perfect verbs. ('Mary had been living in India.' 'Colin had been bed-bound for years.')

- Bring the class back together and invite pairs to read aloud their sentences.

Differentiation
Support: Provide pairs with sentences in the simple past tense and challenge them to convert them to past perfect verbs.

Extension: Let pairs draft paragraphs about Mary or Colin using as many past perfect verbs as they can.

5. How likely?

Objective
To use modal verbs to indicate degrees of possibility.

What you need
Copies of *The Secret Garden*, Extract 3, photocopiable page 23 'How likely?'

What to do

- Re-read Extract 3. Briefly review how and why Mary and Colin have changed. Ask: *Were they aware of what they needed to do to change?*

- Write two sentences on the board: 'Mary could be happier if she stopped thinking bad thoughts.' 'Colin could get better if he stopped thinking about dying.'

- Circle the modal verb 'could'. Ask: *What does the verb suggest?* (that there is a possibility that Mary and Colin will get better but it depends on them changing their thoughts/attitudes)

- List on the board the modal verbs: 'will', 'would', 'may', 'might', 'shall', 'should', 'can', 'could'. Tell the children that we use these verbs to indicate that something is possible and how likely it is.

- Arrange the children into pairs. Let them take turns reading aloud the sentences on the board, experimenting with modal verbs to see which ones make the outcome sound most likely and which least likely. Tell them that they may need to change the tense of the verb in the 'if' clause: 'Mary <u>will</u> be happier if she <u>stops</u> thinking disagreeable thoughts.' 'Colin <u>can</u> get better if he <u>stops</u> thinking about dying.'

- Hand out photocopiable page 23 'How likely?', and let pairs complete it.

Differentiation
Support: Experiment with the modal verbs together before challenging children to complete the photocopiable page.

Extension: Let children discuss how choosing different modal verbs changes the meaning of the sentences on the photocopiable page.

6. Useful brackets

Objective
To use brackets to indicate parenthesis.

What you need
Copies of *The Secret Garden*, photocopiable page 24 'Useful brackets'.

What to do

- Tell the children that you are going to read out some sentences taken from the novel and that they are going to write them down. They should consider punctuation: where to use capital letters, commas, brackets or other punctuation marks to help make sense of the sentence.

- Dictate, at a measured pace, the sentences beginning: 'He could speak robin...' and 'If you have to fly about...' from Chapter 25.

- When the children have had time to check their sentences, refer back to the book and write the sentences in full on the board. Let the children correct their own work. Circle the brackets. Point out that the words before them can stand alone as a complete sentence (they each have a subject and verb). Encourage the children to think what the punctuation marks do (they frame an explanation or clarification).

- Hand out photocopiable page 24 'Useful brackets' and let the children complete it in pairs.

Differentiation
Support: Provide explanations for any tricky words before children complete the task.

Extension: Let children try composing short sentences using tricky words from the novel and including explanations framed by brackets.

Expanding nouns

- Match each phrase to a noun to compose an expanded noun phrase that is used in the novel.

- Draw a line between the phrase and the noun it describes.

The sweetest, most mysterious-looking	hypochondriac
Crabbed old	child
Newly turned	face
A curious loud	place
A hysterical, half-crazy little	sound
The most disagreeable-looking	earth

- Choose one noun from the list above. Compose your own expanded noun phrase, using it in a sentence about the novel.

_____

_____

_____

_____

How likely?

- Choose a modal verb from the box to fill the gap in each sentence.
- Make sure that the verb tense in the 'if' clause works correctly with the verb you choose and change it if necessary.

will	would	may	might	shall	should	can	could

Mary _____ make friends if she stops hating everyone.

Colin _____ become an athlete if he trained hard.

Mrs Medlock _____ sack Martha if she found out about Mary and Colin.

Ben Weatherstaff _____ be angry if he saw Mary go into the garden.

Dr Craven _____ inherit Misselthwaite Manor if Colin dies.

Mr Craven _____ feel better if he went home to see Colin.

Choose two of the sentences and re-write them changing the verb tense of the 'if' clause then add a different modal verb to fit.

1. _____

_____

2. _____

_____

Useful brackets

- Expand each sentence using a phrase in brackets to explain or comment on the tricky word.

A brougham _____ stood waiting for their journey.

Dickon said the roses were wick _____ and would flower again.

Colin was a hypochondriac _____ and only Mary could help him.

Mary remembered the fakirs _____ who repeated words over and over.

Dickon sang the doxology _____ as they gathered around.

- Now write your own sentence using a phrase in brackets to explain or comment on another tricky word from the novel.

_____

_____

_____

_____

PLOT, CHARACTER & SETTING ▶

1. Turning points

Objective
To summarise the main ideas drawn from more than one paragraph, identifying key details that support the main ideas.

What you need
Copies of *The Secret Garden*, photocopiable page 29 'Turning points'.

What to do

- Begin by challenging the children to summarise the plot of the novel in five or six bullet points. Write them in brief on the board: 'Mary moves to live with her uncle'; 'Mary finds the key to the garden'; 'Mary discovers her cousin Colin' and so on.

- Discuss how most novels are a mixture of action and description. Consider that some novels in the adventure and science-fiction genres may be action-packed. In comparison the plot of *The Secret Garden* is relatively simple but there is a lot of descriptive writing: description of the garden, the natural world and the seasons, and of the main characters and how they change. There are nevertheless key turning points which develop the narrative. Explain to the children that they are going to identify the turning points that drive the events or action in the novel.

- Hand out photocopiable page 29 'Turning points' and let the children work in pairs to complete it. When they have finished, bring the class back together and invite pairs to read their summaries, encouraging feedback on which are the most concise and effective.

Differentiation
Support: Briefly discuss the context of each turning point before pairs complete the task.

Extension: Challenge pairs to extend their work by identifying other key turning points.

2. Mistress Mary

Objective
To draw inferences such as inferring characters' feelings, thoughts and motives from their actions, and justifying inferences with evidence.

What you need
Copies of *The Secret Garden*.

What to do

- Tell the children that they are going to focus on the character of Mary. Write on the board three headings: 'Description', 'Dialogue', 'Action'. Suggest to them that authors can use any or all of these to convey a character.

- Arrange the children into small groups and assign them four to five chapters each. Tell them to skim and scan their chapters for examples of description, dialogue and action that help convey Mary's character. Before they begin, read aloud examples for each category, reflecting in each case what they tell us about Mary. 'Mary was an odd, determined little person, and now she had something interesting to be determined about, she was very much absorbed, indeed' (description). '"Who is going to dress me?" demanded Mary' (dialogue). 'She opened the door of the room and went into the corridor, and then she began her wanderings' (action).

- Each group should nominate a note-taker to write down their examples. Bring the class back together and invite volunteers from each group to read aloud their examples. Discuss which are the most effective in conveying Mary's character, encouraging children to support their answers with reasons.

Differentiation
Support: Skim and scan the first chapter together, looking for examples from each category before groups begin.

Extension: Challenge children to compose their own sentences about Mary under each heading.

PLOT, CHARACTER & SETTING

3. From India to England

Objective
To make comparisons within and across books.

What you need
Copies of *The Secret Garden*.

Cross-curricular links
History, geography

What to do

- Tell the children that they are going to focus on the two main settings for the novel: India, and Yorkshire in England.

- Before they begin, remind them that the novel is set in the early 1900s, when India was under the rule of the British Empire. Tell them that this period of rule is known as the British Raj and it lasted from 1858 to 1947, when India gained independence.

- Arrange the children into pairs and tell them to skim and scan the first chapter of the novel, noting down key facts about Mary's life in India. Prompt them by writing questions on the board: 'Why is Mary living in India?' 'What do we know about her home?' 'Who lives there?' They should add their own ideas by speculating: what the weather is like, what the daily routine might be, what the meals are like and who serves them.

- Allow pairs to repeat the exercise focusing on Mary's life in England, using the same question prompts and speculations.

- When they have finished, challenge pairs to use their notes to draw up a comparison chart, using headings such as home, surroundings, weather, servants.

Differentiation
Support: Complete the comparison task as a shared activity.

Extension: Let pairs use their own research on both settings to add facts about weather/climate, surroundings.

4. Dr Craven's case notes

Objective
To use further organisational and presentational devices to structure text and to guide the reader (for example, headings, bullet points, underlining).

What you need
Copies of *The Secret Garden*.

Cross-curricular link
PSHE

What to do

- Tell the children that they are going to imagine that they are Dr Craven, who is in charge of his nephew Colin's health. Ask: *How do the children trick the doctor and staff when Colin is beginning to be restored to health? Why do they do this?* (They pretend he is still very weak so he can surprise his father when he returns.)

- Arrange the children into pairs. Explain to them that they are going to write the doctor's notes following his visits to Colin. They should plan how to structure their notes using dates of visits as headings. On each visit as the doctor, they should record changes they observe – Colin's appearance, weight, behaviour and so on. Here, they could use bullet points or sub headings. Encourage them to include the doctor's feelings – is he puzzled, curious, concerned? Allow them time to draft their notes, then bring the class back together.

- Invite pairs to read aloud their case notes. Discuss why Doctor Craven may have conflicting feelings seeing Colin grow stronger and why he may be puzzled by his recovery. Encourage the children to contrast his approach to Colin's health with that of Susan Sowerby, Mary and Dickon.

Differentiation
Support: Direct children to relevant chapters (19, 24) to find information about Dr Craven's visits.

Extension: Let children develop their notes into a report produced by Dr Craven for Archibald on his return.

5. Moor moods

Objective
To make comparisons within books.

What you need
Copies of *The Secret Garden*, Extract 4.

Cross-curricular link
Geography

What to do

- Tell the children that they are going to focus on the novel's main setting: the Yorkshire moors. Brainstorm some words and phrases describing how Mary sees the moors when she first arrives (dark, desolate, bleak, wind-swept). Ask: *How does she see the moors by the end of the novel?* (exciting, exhilarating, alive) *Who or what has changed the way she sees them?* (Dickon and the way they change with the seasons)

- Arrange the children into pairs. Tell them that they are going to contrast the moors in winter and summer. One child from each pair should make notes describing the moors in winter. The other should make notes describing the moors in summer. They can refer back to the novel and Extract 4 for ideas but they should also use their imaginations and consider the five senses of sight, sound, smell, touch and taste. Before they begin to work independently, brainstorm a few initial ideas together, noting them on the board, for example: the whistling wind in winter, the fluting birds in summer (sound); a dark expanse in winter, the flowering gorse in summer (sight).

- When they have finished, bring the class back together. List the best ideas on the board under the headings 'Winter' and 'Summer'. Challenge pairs to draft a few sentences describing the moors in winter and in summer.

Differentiation
Support: Limit the task to making descriptive notes and compose sentences as a shared activity.

Extension: Let pairs draft a paragraph describing how the seasons change the mood of the moors.

6. Uncle Archibald

Objective
To draw inferences such as inferring characters' feelings, thoughts and motives from their actions, and justifying inferences with evidence.

What you need
Copies of *The Secret Garden*, photocopiable page 30 'Uncle Archibald'.

Cross-curricular link
PSHE

What to do

- Tell the children to focus on the character of Archibald Craven. Ask: *Can you recall why Mary is sent to live with him after her parents die?* (He is her uncle, her mother's brother.) *What are her first impressions of him when she arrives?* (She thinks he does not want to see her; she has heard he is a reclusive hunchback.)

- Arrange the children into pairs and hand out photocopiable page 30 'Uncle Archibald'. Explain that they should read each statement about Mr Craven and decide if it is true or false, then briefly explain why. Allow the children time to complete the task then bring the class back together, asking volunteers to read out their explanations. Suggest that we change our opinion of him as the novel progresses and we learn more about him.

- Invite children to contrast how Mary views Mr Craven when she first arrives at Misselthwaite and how she views him at the end of the story. Let pairs try drafting statements that she might make before and after she really gets to know him. Discuss what made Mr Craven so unhappy (the death of his wife). Ask: *What changes him?* (He begins to replace his dark thoughts with hope.)

Differentiation
Support: Provide chapter or page references to help children find the relevant detail.

Extension: Let pairs draft a short character profile of Mr Craven.

7. Passing time

Objective
To identify how language, structure and presentation contribute to meaning.

What you need
Copies of *The Secret Garden*, photocopiable page 31 'Passing time'.

Cross-curricular link
Science

What to do

- Begin by asking the children how much time they think passes in the story – days, weeks, months or years? Encourage them to support their answers with evidence (the description of the four changing seasons; Mr Craven goes away for a few months until the autumn).

- Ask: *What tells us that time is passing during the novel?* Focus on the idea of change. Ask: *Who or what changes during the course of the story?* (Mary, Colin, Mr Craven, the garden) List them on the board.

- Arrange the children into pairs and hand out photocopiable page 31 'Passing time'. Explain that pairs should discuss and make brief notes on how and why each thing or person changes during the course of the story. When they have finished, bring the class back together and invite pairs to summarise the changes that take place during the story.

- Discuss what links all the changes: the idea of blossoming, growing, coming back to life. Encourage the children to consider how the idea of restoration – the restoration of a garden and of the children as well as Mr Craven – gives the plot structure and shape.

Differentiation
Support: Perform the task as a shared activity, making notes on the board.

Extension: Invite pairs to construct a mind map, plotting the different examples of growth and restoration.

8. It's magic!

Objective
To identify and discuss themes and conventions in and across a wide range of writing.

What you need
Copies of *The Secret Garden*.

What to do

- Tell the children that they are going to focus on the idea of 'magic' and how it helps to shape the narrative.

- Discuss what they understand by the concept of the 'magic' in the novel (the power of positive thoughts, a kind of life force which comes from a benevolent creator). Tell the children that this theme was inspired by the author's study of the Christian Science and New Thought movement which emerged in the 19th century. Both believed in the power of positive thought and the divinity found in the natural world.

- Write on the board: 'Mary', 'Colin', 'Mr Craven'.

- Arrange the children into small groups and allocate one character to each group. Tell them to discuss how 'magic' affects their character's life. Bring the class back together and invite groups to contribute their ideas.

- Using their suggestions, explore together as a class how key events in the narrative are driven by 'magic'. (Through the robin, it is Magic that helps Mary discover the secret garden; it is Magic that helps Colin get to his feet in front of Ben Weatherstaff – and distracts Colin just when Mary and Dickon need it; it is Magic that changes Mr Craven's mood and brings him home to England.)

Differentiation
Support: Let groups focus on how 'magic' drives key events in the narrative.

Extension: Encourage groups to explore 'magic' in relation to other topics or characters: the secret garden, Susan Sowerby, Dickon.

Turning points

- Briefly explain how each of the following represents a turning point in the plot.

1. A cholera epidemic

_____

_____

_____

_____

2. A broken tree

_____

_____

_____

_____

3. A rusty key

_____

_____

_____

_____

4. A train journey home

_____

_____

_____

_____

5. A letter from Yorkshire

Mr Archibald Craven

_____

_____

_____

6. Blue forget-me-nots

_____

_____

_____

_____

Uncle Archibald

- Read the following statements about Archibald Craven and decide if each one is true or false.

- Briefly explain your decision, giving your evidence.

Statement	True/False	Explanation
He is horrid.		
He is a hunchback.		
He is handsome.		
He is lonely.		
He hates his son Colin.		
He is generous.		

 # Passing time

- Make notes explaining the changes that occur in the story and what helps bring them about.

What changes?	How does it change?	What brings about the change?
The garden		
Mary		
Colin		
Mr Craven		

TALK ABOUT IT ▶

1. What are they like?

Objective
To speak audibly and fluently with an increasing command of Standard English.

What you need
Copies of *The Secret Garden*, photocopiable page 35 'What are they like?'

Cross-curricular link
PSHE

What to do
- Tell the children that they are going to focus on adult characters in the story, in particular, the children's parents. Write the name 'Archibald Craven' on the board. Ask the children to describe Mr Craven's character by giving them time to rehearse short statements about him, citing evidence to back them up. (Mr Craven is sad because his wife has died; Mr Craven is generous because he buys Mary gifts.)
- Encourage them to describe both positive and negative aspects of his character. For example, he takes Mary in and provides her with a comfortable home but he has neglected his son Colin.
- Arrange the children into pairs. Hand out photocopiable page 35 'What are they like?' and allow them time to complete it, referring back to the novel where necessary.
- Bring the class back together and invite volunteers from pairs to read aloud their sentences. Challenge children to guess which character is being talked about, and by whom.
- Finish the discussion by considering the impact Mrs Lennox and Mr Craven have on their children, Mary and Colin, in the way they have brought them up and how they have behaved towards them.

Differentiation
Support: Brainstorm words to describe each character before children begin the activity.

Extension: Invite children to use the same model to describe other characters in the story, challenging their writing partner to deduce the speaker and the character.

2. Connect with nature!

Objective
To maintain attention and participate actively in collaborative conversations, staying on topic and initiating and responding to comments.

What you need
Copies of *The Secret Garden*.

Cross-curricular links
PSHE, geography

What to do
- Begin by discussing what helps to make Mary and Colin healthier and happier (nature, being outdoors, the garden). Tell them that recent studies have shown that connecting with nature, being outside in green spaces ('forest bathing'), has a positive effect on mental and physical well-being (mind and body). Explain that many people today live in towns and cities, do indoor jobs and spend work and leisure time on screens. They have lost the connection with nature and the evidence is that their health is suffering.
- Arrange the children into small groups. Challenge them to produce a five-point plan to encourage children of their age to reconnect with nature. They should think about local resources (parks, woods, farms) and devise activities that would encourage children to get out and explore nature and wildlife. Encourage them to discuss how much time children should spend outdoors, how to fit that into their normal daily routine, and how to persuade them to replace screen time with enjoying the outdoors.
- Bring the class back together and invite volunteers from each group to present their plans, encouraging constructive feedback.

Differentiation
Support: Provide a list of local places and resources to prompt ideas.

Extension: Let groups plan a social media campaign to launch and promote their plan.

3. Think positive

> ## Objective
> To use spoken language to develop understanding through speculating, hypothesising, imagining and exploring ideas.
> ## What you need
> Copies of *The Secret Garden*, Extract 3.
> ## Cross-curricular links
> RE, PSHE

What to do

- Re-read Extract 3. Focus on the first paragraph and remind the children that the author was influenced by two belief systems founded in America in the 19th century. Christian Science, which is based on the Bible, believes in healing through prayer. New Thought believes that all illness begins in the mind as the result of bad thoughts, and healing comes from opening the mind to 'divine wisdom'. Ask: *What does the author call this kind of healing in the novel?* (Magic)

- Explore the ways we use positive thinking today, for example, sports psychologists train athletes to focus on targets and to challenge negative thinking. Tell the children that one way to practise positive thinking is to repeat or chant a mantra (an Indian term for a positive statement or affirmation). Mantras are often chanted, aloud or silently, as a meditation technique. Colin's affirmation that he will 'live forever and ever' replaces the thoughts of death which have haunted him.

- Let children work individually to devise three mantras to enhance their own well-being. Encourage them to be concise and focus on how they *want* to feel. Allow them time to practise saying their mantras silently to themselves, noting how they feel.

> ## Differentiation
> **Support:** Model short mantras on the board to get children started ('I am strong; I feel calm').
>
> **Extension:** Allow children time to develop their own positive-thinking plan, challenging negative thoughts.

4. Past times

> ## Objective
> To give well-structured descriptions, explanations and narratives for different purposes, including for expressing feelings.
> ## What you need
> Copies of *The Secret Garden*, photocopiable page 36 'Past times'.
> ## Cross-curricular link
> History

What to do

- Tell the children that they are going to consider the period setting of the novel (the early 20th century). Ask: *What tells us that the story is set in the past?* Brainstorm some ideas of evidence, noting initial ideas on the board (transport, clothes, households, communications).

- Arrange the children into pairs and hand out photocopiable page 36 'Past times'. Read through each heading, prompting with questions. For example, ask: *How does Mary travel to Misselthwaite Manor?* (transport); *Who lives at the manor and who works there?* (households); *How do the children speak to the servants?* (manners/language); *How does Mrs Sowerby contact Mr Craven when he is abroad?* (communications) Tell the children to skim and scan the novel to help them complete the task.

- Bring the class back together and share their ideas. Discuss how the novel is a 'period piece', reflecting attitudes of the early 1900s. Explore the idea that some of the attitudes and manners of the period (for example, towards Indian peoples or servants) are offensive and no longer acceptable today.

> ## Differentiation
> **Support:** Write a list of ideas on the board and challenge pairs to cite evidence from the text.
>
> **Extension:** Encourage children to investigate ideas in other classics such as Charles Kingsley's *The Water Babies* which may not be acceptable today.

⬇ **TALK ABOUT IT**

5. Masters and servants

Objective
To participate in discussions and debates.
What you need
Copies of *The Secret Garden*, photocopiable page 37 'Masters and servants'.
Cross-curricular link
History

What to do

- Tell the children that they are going to think about all the people that Mr Craven employs at Misselthwaite Manor and the roles they have in the running of the household. Remind them that the novel is set in the early 1900s. Explain that before the First World War (1914–18) wealthy people would employ servants including maids, cooks and gardeners to look after their houses and gardens.

- Arrange the children into pairs and hand out photocopiable page 37 'Masters and servants'. Explain that they should fill in the names of all Mr Craven's employees, for example, Head Gardener: Mr Roach, Housekeeper: Mrs Medlock and so on.

- They should then write notes showing what each person's work for Mr Craven involves, referring back to the novel to help them.

- When they have finished, bring the class back together for a discussion about the master-servant relationship as shown in the novel. Ask: *How are the servants treated/spoken to? What threat do they face if they upset their master or mistress?* (losing their job) Explore how things have changed today, when people are employed to work in houses or gardens.

Differentiation
Support: Provide a list of names and let children assign them to the correct roles.

Extension: Let pairs of children carry out their own research to find out more about servants working 'below stairs' in the early 1900s.

6. Yorkshire speak

Objective
To select and use appropriate registers for effective communication.
What you need
Copies of *The Secret Garden*.

What to do

- Tell the children that they are going to focus on the Yorkshire dialect that the author uses in the novel. Ask: *Why does the author use dialect for characters like Ben Weatherstaff and Dickon?* (to help create a sense of place and character)

- Discuss how Mary's views of Yorkshire change in the novel. At first she can't understand Martha's words, but later she learns to speak Yorkshire and teaches it to Colin. Ask: *Why does she like it?* (It is natural, easy; it represents the people she has become fond of.)

- Write the Yorkshire word 'wuthering' on the board and ask a volunteer to explain what it means (used to describe windy conditions). List on the board some typical features of a dialect: special words, different pronunciations, non-standard use of words and grammar.

- Read aloud Dickon's words (Chapter 15) beginning '"We munnot stir,"' as far as '"us'll not be in his way."' Analyse the text, highlighting verbs ('knowed', 'seed') missing letters ('buildin', 'th') and pronouns ('us').

- Arrange the children into pairs. Challenge them to change Dickon's words into Standard English. When they have finished, invite volunteers to read aloud the two versions of dialogue. Review how the dialect helps convey Dickon's character.

Differentiation
Support: Perform the task as a shared activity, working through the words together.

Extension: Let pairs choose another passage of dialect to translate into Standard English.

What are they like?

- Write a statement about each of these characters from the point of view of other characters from the story. Begin each statement with the pronoun 'He' or 'She' and back up your statement with reasons.

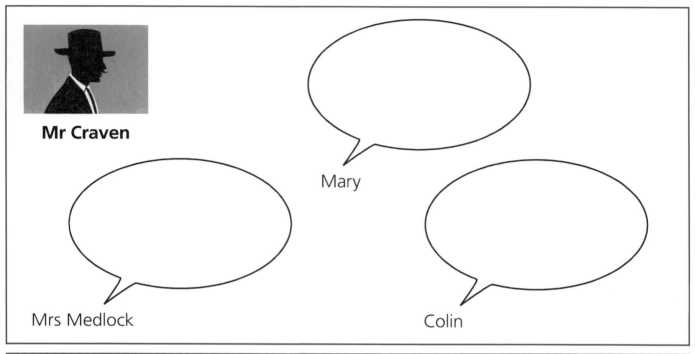

Mr Craven

Mary

Mrs Medlock

Colin

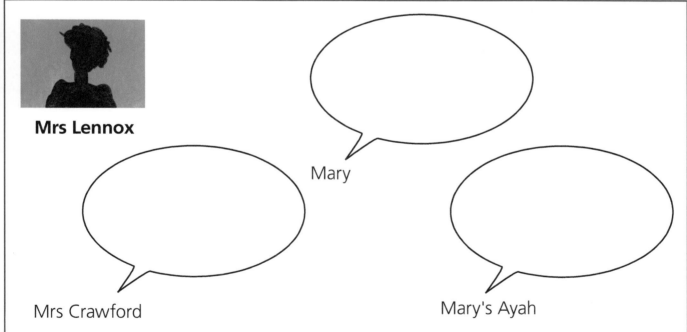

Mrs Lennox

Mary

Mrs Crawford

Mary's Ayah

Choose adjectives from the box below or think of your own.

| generous | cold | caring | sad | selfish | uncaring | kind | thoughtful | wise |

 # Past times

- For each category, find and write down evidence from the text that tells us that the story is set in the past.

Transport

_____

_____

_____

_____

Clothes

_____

_____

_____

_____

_____

Households

_____

_____

_____

_____

_____

Manners/language

_____

_____

_____

_____

_____

Communications

_____

_____

_____

_____

Masters and servants

- Fill in the names of Mr Craven's servants and employees. Write brief notes on what their work involves.

The Household of Archibald Craven, Misselthwaite Manor

Housekeeper
_____
_____
_____

Housemaid
_____
_____
_____

Head gardener
_____
_____
_____

Under-gardener
_____
_____
_____

Doctor
_____
_____
_____
_____

GET WRITING ▶

1. Opening scenes

Objective
To summarise the main ideas drawn from more than one paragraph.

What you need
Copies of *The Secret Garden*, photocopiable page 41 'Opening scenes'.

Cross-curricular link
Art and design

What to do

- Re-read Chapter 1. Discuss how the opening chapter is dramatic and fast moving. Challenge the children to summarise the main events (Mary is orphaned and left alone in the bungalow in India when cholera kills her family and their household servants). Ask: *How do you think Mary is feeling?* (alone, confused, angry)

- Tell the children to imagine that they are preparing to film the scene for a movie using a storyboard or sequence of pictures showing how the action develops. Write on the board the headings: 'Characters', 'Setting', 'Action' and remind the children that each scene in a storyboard needs to summarise who appears, where the scene is set, and what happens.

- Hand out photocopiable page 41 'Opening scenes' and arrange the children into pairs. Tell them to skim and scan Chapter 1 to decide on four scenes to brief. They should write notes for each scene on the photocopiable page. Encourage them to include detail such as sound effects (the servants wailing, approaching footsteps) and ideas for close-up camera shots (the unfinished food and wine, the snake slithering across the floor, Mary's frightened face).

- Bring the class back together and write the best suggestions on the board.

- Let the children, in their pairs, sketch the storyboard scenes they have briefed.

2. Letters about Mary

Objective
To plan their writing by identifying the audience for and purpose of the writing, selecting the appropriate form and using other similar writing as models for their own.

What you need
Copies of *The Secret Garden*.

What to do

- Ask a volunteer to summarise how Mary comes to be living at Misselthwaite Manor. Ask: *Can you suggest how Mr Craven would have been informed, considering when the novel is set?* (by letter)

- Tell the children that they are going to draft a letter sent to Mr Craven by a government official in India, informing him of Mary's situation. Revise some of the key features of letter writing, including layout. Emphasise that this is a formal letter so the language and grammar need to be appropriate.

- Invite the children to begin by noting down key information the letter needs to contain. Suggest they re-read Mr Craven's words to Mrs Medlock informing her what has happened. Note key ideas on the board: Mr and Mrs Lennox have died during a cholera epidemic, their daughter Mary is an orphan, Mr Craven is her guardian and so on.

- Using the notes, let the children draft a letter to be sent to Mr Craven. When they have finished, invite volunteers to read aloud their letters. Consider together if the letter is clear, if it contains the necessary information and if the tone and language are appropriate.

Differentiation
Support: Let children work in pairs to draft a letter.

Extension: Challenge children to write Mr Craven's reply.

3. Mary's diary

Objective
To identify the audience for and purpose of the writing, selecting the appropriate form and using other similar writing as models for their own.

What you need
Copies of *The Secret Garden*.

What to do

- Read together Chapter 6. Tell the children that they are going to focus on the rainy day and write a diary entry that Mary might write, describing all the things that she does to amuse herself, and what she discovers when she explores the manor house.

- Arrange the children into pairs. Tell them to skim and scan the chapter, making notes on all the events that happen on the rainy day (Mary decides to explore the house, she plays with the ivory elephants, she finds the nesting mouse, Mary gets caught by Mrs Medlock). Encourage them to think how Mary is feeling (bored, curious about the crying, angry with Mrs Medlock).

- Let the children use their notes to work individually to write a diary entry. They should include details like the weather (pouring rain and mist) and how the day began (talking to Martha). Allow them time to complete their entries, then read them to their writing partners, comparing and contrasting the content. Encourage constructive feedback.

Differentiation
Support: Scan the chapter together, making notes on the board, then ask children to draft a diary entry.

Extension: Challenge children to write a diary entry for another day or another character from the novel.

4. Susan's rules

Objective
To use organisational and presentational devices to structure text and to guide the reader (headings, bullet points, underlining).

What you need
Copies of *The Secret Garden*.

Cross-curricular link
PSHE

What to do

- Tell the children that they are going to focus on the character of Dickon's mother, Susan Sowerby. Brainstorm some adjectives to describe her and write them on the board (motherly, kind, caring, warm). Ask: *What do other characters say or think about her?* (Colin wishes she were his mother; Martha says she is sensible, hard-working and good natured; Mary finds her comforting.)

- Arrange the children into pairs. Challenge them to make a guide or a set of instructions summarising Susan's views on bringing up children. They should refer back to the text and list their ideas.

- Model one or two ideas on the board, showing how instructions can take different forms: 'Children must have good healthy food' or 'Feed children good healthy food', 'Children must be allowed to play and roam free' or 'Let children play and roam free', 'Children must feel wanted and loved' or 'Make children feel wanted and loved'.

- Encourage them to think how to organise their guide: will they list using bullet points, numbers or letters? Will they use headings such as food, playtime, learning skills?

- Allow them time to draft their guides then invite volunteers to present their ideas.

Differentiation
Support: Read key passages together before children begin work.

Extension: Discuss as a class how many of Susan's rules apply today and how some might need to be adapted.

5. Go figurative!

Objective
To discuss and evaluate how authors use language, including figurative language, considering the impact on the reader.

What you need
Copies of *The Secret* Garden, photocopiable page 42 'Go figurative!'

What to do
- Tell the children that they are going to focus on the author's language and, in particular, her use of figurative language, including similes and metaphors. Read together the beginning of Chapter 7, as far as '…awful dreary grey'. Ask: *Can you find a simile and a metaphor?* ('like the waters of some lovely bottomless lake' (simile), 'small clouds of snow-white fleece' (metaphor))

- Encourage the children to consider how the comparisons help the reader imagine the scene and how much more effective the simile and metaphor are than saying simply 'the sky was a deep blue' and 'the clouds were fluffy and white'. Point out that, in each case, the author has chosen to evoke other features of landscapes, the deep blue of a lake and the white of snow and sheep's wool.

- Hand out photocopiable page 42 'Go figurative!' and let children work in pairs to complete it. When they have finished, bring the class back together to review their work. Ask: *Which phrases do you find most effective and why?*

- Challenge pairs to write their own sentences using a simile or a metaphor to describe three things that Mary sees when she enters the garden.

Differentiation
Extension: Challenge pairs to write more sentences containing similes or metaphors describing characters or places in the novel.

6. A Yorkshire poem

Objective
To note and develop initial ideas, drawing on reading and research where necessary.

What you need
Copies of *The Secret Garden*, photocopiable page 43 'A Yorkshire poem'.

Cross-curricular link
Drama

What to do
- Invite the children to recall some dialect words that feature in the novel and write them on the board (for example, 'wuthering', 'graidely', 'wick'). Consider each word and challenge them to explain the word's meaning and identify the part of speech, suggesting a short sentence to bring out the meaning.

- Tell the children that they are going to choose one or more of the dialect words and try to write a short poem about a topic from the novel using those words. Brainstorm a few ideas to get them started: the wind on the moors, spring in the garden, bulbs in the soil.

- Hand out photocopiable page 43 'A Yorkshire poem' and explain that they should use the sheet to plan their poem. Revise the terms 'simile' and 'metaphor' by providing examples from the text (such as 'a loose and swinging curtain' to describe the curtain of ivy).

- When they have finished, allow them time to draft and edit their poems. Invite volunteers to read their poems to the class and encourage constructive feedback. Ask: *Which poems are most effective and why? Which reflect something described in the novel best?*

Differentiation
Support: Write some dialect words on the board and brainstorm initial ideas for poems.

Extension: Challenge children to brief a presentation or dramatisation of their poem for radio, considering tone, volume, intonation, music and sound effects.

Opening scenes

- Write a storyboard brief for four scenes for the opening sequence of a film of *The Secret Garden*. Don't forget to include your ideas for sound effects and close-ups.

Scene 1	Scene 2
Characters: _____ _____ _____	Characters: _____ _____ _____
Setting: _____ _____ _____	Setting: _____ _____ _____
Action: _____ _____ _____ _____	Action: _____ _____ _____ _____
Scene 3	**Scene 4**
Characters: _____ _____ _____	Characters: _____ _____ _____
Setting: _____ _____ _____	Setting: _____ _____ _____
Action: _____ _____ _____ _____	Action: _____ _____ _____ _____

GET WRITING

Go figurative!

- Draw a line to match a subject to the phrase that describes it. Then write a sentence on the line next to the phrase to explain the comparison.

branches and sprays	with eyes like jewels
a wheeled chair	a wide expanse of black ocean
the moor	a loose and swinging curtain
ivy	some sort of state coach
snake	a sort of hazy mantle

A Yorkshire poem

• Use this sheet to plan a poem about a topic from the novel using at least one Yorkshire dialect word.

The Yorkshire dialect word/s I will use is: _____

_____

_____

_____

Meaning of word/s: _____

_____

_____

_____

_____

My poem will be about: _____

_____

_____

_____

_____

A simile or metaphor I will use in my poem is: _____

_____

_____

_____

_____

ASSESSMENT ▶

1. Time for a test

Objective
To ask questions to improve their understanding.

What you need
Copies of *The Secret Garden*.

What to do

- Tell the children that they are going to compile multiple-choice quiz questions about the novel to challenge other groups or teams. Arrange them into small groups and allow time for them to compile a quiz of six multiple-choice questions. Children should skim and scan the novel for ideas for their questions. They should appoint one note-taker to write down their questions and another to keep a list of correct answers.

- Before they begin, model an example of a multiple choice question on the board.

- Once everyone has finished, groups can then challenge each other to answer their quiz questions. Again, they will need to appoint a note-taker to count correct answers. When they have finished, review the scores and announce the winning teams or groups.

- Encourage feedback, identifying which quiz questions were most challenging and why (for example, where the names of characters or animals could be confused).

Differentiation
Support: Ask children to rehearse their questions with you before quizzing the class to ensure their answers are accurate.

Extension: Let groups devise an alternative quiz such as a true or false quiz about the novel to challenge other groups.

2. First impressions

Objective
To provide reasoned justifications for their views.

What you need
Copies of *The Secret Garden*, photocopiable page 47 'First impressions'.

Cross-curricular link
PSHE

What to do

- Write the name 'Mary' on the board. Ask: *Can you suggest adjectives that characters in the novel might use to describe Mary?* (disagreeable, contrary, rude) Challenge the children to give their reasons, for example, Martha thinks Mary is rude because of the way she speaks to her.

- Next, challenge the children to come up with adjectives which describe what Mary is like underneath, qualities that people might not see at first but which she begins to reveal during the novel (lonely, determined, kind). Again, they should use the adjectives in sentences to explain their choices. For example, Mary is determined because she starts tending the garden on her own.

- Arrange the class into small groups. Assign each group another character: Colin, Archibald Craven or Ben Weatherstaff. Challenge them to repeat both parts of the exercise for their character, then bring the class back together and invite volunteers from each group to suggest sentences. Hand out photocopiable page 47 'First impressions' and let the children complete it, working individually.

- When they have finished, share ideas and discuss how first impressions of characters can be wrong: for example, Archibald Craven may seem cold and distant but underneath he is lonely and unhappy.

Differentiation
Support: Let children work in pairs to complete the photocopiable page.

3. A Yorkshire glossary

Objectives
To check that the book makes sense to them, discussing their understanding and exploring the meaning of words in context; to use brackets, dashes or commas to indicate parenthesis.

What you need
Copies of *The Secret Garden*, dictionaries.

Cross-curricular links
Geography, history

What to do

- Tell the children that they are going to compile a glossary of Yorkshire words which will help readers understand the local dialect that Mary learns to speak.

- Arrange the children into small groups and assign each group four to five chapters (beginning with Chapter 2). Ask them to skim and scan their chapters for any dialect words (for example, 'graidely', 'nesh', 'wuthering', 'nowt', 'marred'). They should also include dialect forms of familiar words such as 'mun', 'munnot' (must, must not).

- They should appoint a note-taker to list all the words they can find.

- When the groups have finished, let them use their word lists to test other groups on spellings and meanings. The children can then share their findings to compile a glossary of Yorkshire dialect words.

- Challenge children to choose a word from the glossary and write a sentence using that word. They should also include a definition in parenthesis (using brackets, commas or dashes) to explain its meaning clearly to readers. For example, Mrs Medlock thought Mary was marred (spoiled).

Differentiation
Support: Allow children to use online dialect dictionaries to help them compile their glossaries.

Extension: Challenge groups to use their own research to extend their glossaries.

4. Top themes

Objective
To identify and discuss themes and conventions in and across a wide range of writing.

What you need
Copies of *The Secret Garden*.

Cross-curricular link
PSHE

What to do

- Ask: *What are the main themes in the novel?* (the healing power of nature, the power of positive thinking, the fact that love nourishes and neglect weakens) Write the children's ideas on the board, prompting them with questions as necessary. Ask: *What does the author suggest about gardens and nature? What does she suggest causes illness and unhappiness?*

- If the children have recently read any other novels that cover similar themes (for example, animal-human friendships), invite comparisons, focussing on key features such as characters, narrative voice, setting, and encourage subjective opinion. Use the prompt 'This novel made me think about…' to structure their thoughts.

- Invite the children to choose the theme they think is most significant or which has most impact on them. They should draft a short statement beginning 'I think *The Secret Garden* is a novel about…' describing the theme and why they think it is important. For example, 'I think *The Secret Garden* is about the healing power of the natural world because Mary and Colin restore the garden and the garden restores them.'

- Invite volunteers to read out their statements and encourage feedback from the rest of the class.

Differentiation
Support: List key themes on the board then ask children to choose the one they think is most significant and draft a statement about it.

Extension: Children can construct mind maps showing how main themes in the novel are connected.

5. Book club

Objective
To give well-structured descriptions, explanations and narratives for different purposes, including for expressing feelings.

What you need
Copies of *The Secret Garden*.

What to do
- Explain to the children that they are going to pretend that they are taking part in a book club programme on the radio to review the novel.

- Discuss some questions that the programme's presenter might ask and list them on the board, for example, 'Did you enjoy the novel and if so why?' 'What is your favourite part of the novel and why?' 'Who is your favourite character?' 'Would this novel encourage you to read others by the same author and, if so, why?'

- Allow the children time to work on their own to prepare some notes on what they think or feel about the novel. Encourage them to refer to the novel and to back up their views with evidence – for example, I like Dickon because he makes friends with all the animals.

- Appoint a presenter or presenters who will give a brief introduction to the book and then invite others to participate in a group discussion about the novel. The presenter can use the questions on the board and add more of their own.

Differentiation
Support: Children could discuss their opinions of the novel in pairs before they begin the book club discussion.

Extension: Children could make their own podcast or create a newspaper review.

6. Chapter and content

Objectives
To summarise the main ideas drawn from more than one paragraph.

What you need
Copies of *The Secret Garden*.

What to do
- Use the author's chapter titles to review the way the novel is structured. Let the children scan the chapter titles. Ask volunteers to pick out some examples to explain the content behind the title - for example, Chapter 10; 'Dickon' introduces the character of Dickon Chapter 14 'A Young Rajah' describes the way Colin behaves like an imperious Indian prince.

- Select some titles at random and challenge volunteers to explain the chapter content that they indicate – for example, Chapter 17 'A Tantrum' describes Colin going into hysterics; Chapter 25 'The Curtain' refers to the curtain that covered the portrait of Colin's mother, which he has now decided is better drawn back.

- Encourage the children to consider what the author's chapter titles contribute, listing their ideas on the board. (The author uses some chapter titles to introduce characters ('Martha', 'Dickon', 'Ben Weatherstaff') and others to give us significant snippets of dialogue ('"I Am Colin"'; '"I Won't!" Said Mary') or she offers us clues to the action which encourage us to wonder or predict what might happen ('The Key to the Garden'; 'Magic').

Differentiation
Support: Focus on the less obvious titles and let children refer back to the novel to interpret references.

Extension: Challenge children to come up with alternative titles for some chapters.

First impressions

- Think of an adjective to complete each sentence and give your reasons for the words you have chosen.

People think Mary is _____ because
_____ .

Underneath Mary feels _____ because
_____ .

People think Colin is _____ because
_____ .

Underneath Colin feels _____ because
_____ .

People think Ben Weatherstaff is _____ because
_____ .

Underneath Ben Weatherstaff feels _____ because
_____ .

People think Archibald Craven is _____ because
_____ .

Underneath Archibald Craven feels _____ because
_____ .

SCHOLASTIC
READ & RESPOND
Available in this series:

Key Stage 1

978-1407-18254-4

978-1407-16053-5

978-1407-14220-3

978-1407-15875-4

978-1407-16058-0

Key Stage 2

978-1407-14228-9

978-1407-14224-1

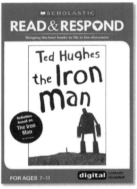

978-1407-14229-6

978-14071-6057-3

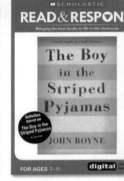

978-14071-6071-9

978-14071-6069-6

978-14071-6067-2

978-14071-4231-9

978-14071-4223-4

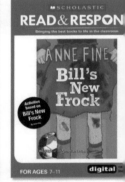

978-14071-6060-3

978-14071-5876-1

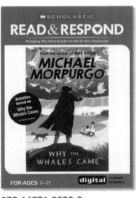

978-14071-6068-9

978-14071-6063-4

978-1407-18253-7

978-1407-18252-0

To find out more, call 0845 6039091
or visit our website www.scholastic.co.uk/readandrespond